When Jesus Rose

WHEN JESUS ROSE

Wallace D. Chappell

BROADMAN PRESS
Nashville, Tennessee

© Copyright 1972 • Broadman Press
All rights reserved
ISBN: 0–8054–2218–8
4222–18

Library of Congress Catalog Card Number: 72–90034
Dewey Decimal Classification: 232.97
Printed in the United States of America

This is dedicated to
Kate and Wallace B. Davis,
dear friends, whose lives
give constant evidence that
he has risen.

Foreword

This book is not a selection of sermons on sporadic texts. It is a series of addresses arranged so as to present the life which Christ gives as a present possession. The purpose of these studies is to set the events following the resurrection and its words in relation to the purpose of Christ's life and death. Wallace Chappell, master of the holy craft, has expounded their teaching for faith and righteousness. The title of the book has been chosen not for the music of its sound, but for the fitness of its meaning. The resurrection was not some far-off event; it was not something for which Christ had to ask the Father; but it was present and actual in himself. Christ offered himself as the answer to men's questions and the final satisfaction of their needs. When the people of Galilee said, "Evermore give us this bread," he said to them, "I am the Bread of Life." When the people were torn and distracted by doubt, not knowing which way to turn, and not knowing what to believe, Christ offered himself as their sufficient guidance, saying, "I am the Light of the world." To the doubts and fears of Martha, he offered himself as the answer: "I am the Resurrection and the Life."

May I express the hope that those who read from the

pen of my friend and brother of many years, Wallace Chappell, will be led to spend some quiet days with Christ, see his glory, feel the need of his grace, and in a renewing dedication of life and service, confess him Lord.

ROBERT J. NORMAN, Pastor
Belmont Heights Baptist Church
Nashville, Tennessee

Preface

There are three phases of our Lord's ministry. There was the three-year interval when he was visibly present. Following Pentecost, there is the spiritual period in which he is invisibly present.

However, there was another second span, a forty-day period (Acts 1:3) when Christ appeared, disappeared, then reappeared.

Dietrich Bonhoeffer once wrote from the Tegel Prison in Berlin, "I have long had a special affection for the season between Easter and the ascension." I must also confess to a particular fondness for this meaningful interlude, this fruitful valley between the two hills of Calvary and the ascension.

These forty days were tremendously significant. Here Christ proved in risen reality he was our everlasting Lord. Then it was during this time that the followers of Jesus were becoming a Spirit-filled fellowship that would some day become the church eternal. These messages speak to this period.

God grant that in these days we too will be filled with his spirit. Let our earnest prayer be that the risen Christ, the Holy Spirit within, will bind us together that he may send us out.

Contents

When Jesus Rose

1

The Compelling Haste

"Go quickly, and tell his disciples that he is risen."
Matthew 28:7

He is risen." Our Lord lives!

Whatever else may be the tidings that our church is sharing with the world, it is not good news until we proclaim Christ is alive. He is our grave-conquering Savior: our eternal Immanuel.

This was the triumphant word the angel of the resurrection gave to the world of twenty centuries ago. It was earthshaking then. It has not lost its power for our day.

Let us look at the full impact of this dynamic declaration.

I

The first aspect of this declaration is the call to act: "Go."

The brief trek the two Marys made back to Jerusalem was the beginning of a journey that would take Christ's followers across the Roman world. And the journey continues today. Some must cross the sea . . . some must

cross the street. Some must climb mountain precipices . . .
some must traverse racial barriers. Some must invade
hazardous cultures . . . others must face indifferent neighbors. But to the varying spheres of need we must direct
our footsteps with the good news that Christ is alive!

To be sure this is not easy. In most local churches any
emphasis draws more participation than the "going out"
of the brotherhood. For many "I shall not be moved,"
remains a favorite hymn. But until the church gathered
becomes the church scattered, we will never reach the
majority of the world's lost and lonely.

I had been preaching in a Bible conference with my
friend, Bishop Arthur J. Moore. On our last evening
together I asked about his preaching schedule. He is
past eighty years of age now, so I thought perhaps he
preached a week and rested a week. "Wallace," he said,
"I don't stop anymore between engagements. I am afraid
if I start going easier I will quit entirely." I do not
know that I quite agree with my friend physically speaking, but in the spiritual connotation he is completely
right. If we die down we die out. "Go," said the angel.
There is no vital religion apart from this action ethic.

The second point of consequence has to do with the
word "quickly." "Go quickly," commanded the angel.

This, too, is a significant issue that needs stress. How
prone we are to be lackadaisical and slothful about the
greatest news ever given to the world. Indeed, we seem
to be in a mad rush to do all else except the one thing
we ought to make haste to do.

I am a great believer in practicing the quiet hour. Our nervous, noisy, neurotic world could well learn a life-changing lesson from our Quaker friends in this realm. But though we must be still and know, we must also be swift and proclaim. "Make haste," said Jesus to Zacchaeus. And that which we have shown speed in experiencing, we must show speed in expressing.

Two laymen went to see a third about making a donation for a proposed church that was much needed in their community. The man told his visitors that he had recently included $10,000 in his will for such a project. His callers expressed their gratitude but indicated the immediate necessity of a church in that area. "Friends," he replied; "I have told you what I have done and this must definitely end the matter. You won't get a penny from me until I'm dead." "Now, my brother," one of the men answered, "don't say that. The Lord knows just how badly we need this church."

There was more than humor in this response. These men felt the compulsion of erecting a building where men might worship and children might learn to pray.

Our Lord knew that often speed is essential. "I must work the works of him that sent me, while it is day:" he said, "the night cometh, when no man can work" (John 9:4).

The third word that is important in the angelic tidings is "tell." This is the motive for action. This is the reason for speed. A sinful world waits for the proclamation of a living Lord. We must not fail to declare this truth.

"This is a day of good news," confessed a quartet in the Old Testament, "and we are not spreading it" (2 Kings 7:9, Moffatt). How many of us could make a similar confession of failure?

"Let us go into the next towns, that I may preach:" said the greatest proclaimer, "for therefore came I forth" (Mark 1:38).

So witnessing is of supreme moment! Our lives are not enough to tell men of his coming and his death and his resurrection. That requires witness.

And we are sharers of the good news. In the New Testament scene of the word, we are all witnesses. How the fellowship needs to be aware that it is not in the main the professional religionists who are entrusted with the task of sharing God's good news. Ninety percent of the members of the churches in our country, for instance, are laymen. I do not know the New Testament ratio, but I do know that for the most part the disciples were untrained witnesses. Peter was a fisherman. Matthew was a tax collector. Barnabas was a farmer. And when one gets right down to occupations, Jesus was a carpenter. Regardless of our vocation, we are good news bringers.

II

Why should we act speedily to declare the news of Christ's resurrection? I think the initial answer is because of the nature of the news itself.

"Fear not;" the angel said to the women, "I know

that ye seek Jesus, which was crucified. He is not here: for he is risen" (Matt. 28:5–6).

Then their darkness became light—their night became day—their fear became faith—their grief became joy. My soul! No wonder they were in a hurry to make known the Easter message.

Come, ye faithful, raise the strain
Of triumphant gladness:
God hath brought His people forth
Into joy from sadness.
Now rejoice, Jerusalem,
And with true affection,
Welcome in unwearied strains
Jesus' resurrection.

'Tis the spring of souls today:
Christ hath burst His prison,
From the frost and gloom of death
Light and life have risen:
All the winter of our sins,
Long and dark, is flying
From His light, to whom we give
Thanks and praise undying.

One simply cannot be apathetic with news like that!

There was once a little girl in a church I served who became desperately ill with spinal meningitis. Sandy seemed especially close to us. She played with our little daughter, who was the same age, and we loved her dearly.

I shall never forget that late night hour when the doctor came to her father and me with the glowing report that Sandy would live. Her mother had gone to the waiting room for a bit of rest. The two of us all but dashed down the hall to convey the glad tidings that life had won.

How can we be indifferent with life's supreme triumph? There is an empty tomb—a living Lord—a victorious faith! We should act swiftly with the news that he has risen, because for many this tremendous truth has never brought the dawn of a new day. Not all of these who do not know are outside the church. Indeed, one of our more able churchmen suggests that perhaps three fourths of all our church people do not know Christ as a risen reality.

"It is one thing to believe in God; it is another thing to confront him," wisely states Harry Emerson Fosdick. "The trouble is not that we think God untrue, but unreal."[1]

A buried Messiah cannot be confronted. Emil Brunner is quite correct when he affirms that "a dead person cannot be your Redeemer."[2]

But a living Lord, our risen Redeemer, brings truth and reality to all of life. Yet, I say again there are countless millions for whom this victorious fact means nothing. It also may be true that for those in prominent positions of leadership in the church all too often our Lord may as well be dust in a Jerusalem grave.

Not long ago I was driving back to my home from Georgia. I came to a spacious farm. There were thousands upon thousands of acres of cotton. I do not know how far I drove before I left the boundary of that particular farm. Yet in all of that land of white, I saw only four people picking cotton.

Jesus said, "The harvest truly is plenteous but the labourers are few." How white the fields! How few the reapers! We will never have a great harvest without until we have his living presence within!

Finally, we should make haste to proclaim Christ's resurrection today because there are some people who will not be here tomorrow.

Hell and death may appear ruthless but they are real. One may ask if we do not have them in the wrong position—should it not be death, then hell? The pathetic thing is that hell often precedes death, and I do not know but that the preceding may be as bad as the succeeding.

Here is a parent who has never lived the Christ-life in front of his child. The boy goes wrong and wastes his youthful years behind prison bars. Does that father have to die to go to hell?

Or here is a mother who taught her child etiquette and culture and fashion. But a social drink was not enough and now she seems hopelessly lost in chronic alcoholism. Does that mother have to die to go to hell?

Or with thousands of opportunities to share the evangel of conquered death we hold back the tidings of truth. Then a pupil dies of leukemia, or a business associate commits suicide, or a neighbor is killed in an accident. And a lifetime of regret follows because we did nothing to prepare them spiritually for eternity. Does one have to die to go to hell?

I am not calling here for prophets of doom. But the Scriptures say, "It is appointed unto men once to die" (Heb. 9:27). This is just as true as John 3:16. We may not wish to think of it or look at it but death is a fact and every day men are dying without hope or faith.

One night in Chicago, Moody told a great congregation that he wanted them to consider what he had preached that evening and the following night he would invite them to make a public stand. But the great fire broke out that very night, and many lives were lost including numbers who attended his services.

Paul said, "Now is the day of salvation" (2 Cor. 6:2), but the opportunity in Chicago was neglected.

Here is an illustration of a young lady who took Paul at his word.

A few years ago I was preaching in one of our large Southern cities. One morning I was invited to a certain high school as chapel speaker. A good many months after that assembly, I was again visiting in that city and preaching in one of the local churches. A call came for me one evening. It was a girl who had attended the school convocation. Her story was at once sad and sordid.

Her parents had both been killed in a car wreck. As a senior in high school she had become a vocalist for an orchestra. She began dating the orchestra leader even though he was married. When she discovered that she was expecting a child, she decided to take her life. It was at this particular time that she attended the chapel service.

She concluded the conversation: "Mr. Chappell, I don't want a thing. I am not asking for a handout. I read in the paper that you were preaching in our city, and I simply wanted to call and tell you I am alive today because you preached in my high school."

A risen Lord meant to this girl the difference between life and death. This is not an hour for delay. God grant that we shall go quickly and tell!

NOTES

1. Harry Emerson Fosdick, *What Is Vital in Religion*
2. Emil Brunner, *I Believe in the Living God*

2

The
Supreme
Mission

"Go and make disciples of all nations, baptize them
in the name of the Father and the Son and the
holy Spirit, and teach them to obey all the commands I have laid on you. And all the time I will
be with you, to the very end of the world."

Matthew 28:19–20, Moffatt

There is a book in my library to which I refer often. It is *The Company of the Committed* by Elton Trueblood. It is one of the outstanding exhortations to the church to be redemptively relevant that has been issued during this decade. Dr. Trueblood calls for the church gathered to be the church scattered in this way: "The only purpose of a company is a campaign."[1] And, of course, he is right. The test of our devotion is our willingness to declare. If our consecration has not led us to proclamation, it would be wise for us to investigate the depth of our spiritual experience. It might be we would find Jesus' words to a certain learned visitor he once had, entirely appropriate to us: "Ye must be born again" (John 3:7).

The scene of our text is on a Galilean mountain. When the disciples saw Jesus, the Scriptures say that "they worshipped him" (Matt. 28:17). Jesus immediately charged them with the task of spreading the gospel in the world. I think it is significant to note he seemed little interested in their worship but wholly concerned with their witness.

Here are his words; "Go and make disciples of all nations, baptize them in the name of the Father and the Son and the holy Spirit, and teach them to obey all the commands I have laid on you. And all the time I will be with you, to the very end of the world" (Matt. 28:19-20, Moffatt).

I

Let us look at our mission in the light of these words. First, Jesus said, "Go." We have *a price to pay*. It would seem, judging from the ministry of our Lord, that he certainly wanted his followers to be aware of the fact that there was a sacrifice involved in discipleship. And he wanted them to know that he felt it was necessary for them to consider that cost.

He spoke on one occasion of building a tower. The first thing the builder should do if he planned to build a tower, was to calculate the expense.

Again, Jesus questioned whether a king would engage another king in combat without first deliberating whether he should face his enemy of twenty thousand men when he had but ten thousand.

One man declared that he would follow Jesus anywhere. However, when Jesus replied that he had nowhere to lay his head, we are not told that this would-be follower enlisted.

Another man, after being urged to follow, informed

Jesus that he would first have to bury his father. Jesus responded by saying: "Let the dead bury their dead: but go thou and preach the kingdom of God" (Luke 9:60). After such a charge, if this man became a recruit, we do not know about it.

Still another announced that he was a candidate for discipleship but that he first had to say good-by to his people at home. Jesus answered by saying: "No man, having put his hand to the plow, and looking back, is fit for the kingdom of God" (Luke 9:62). Evidently such a course of action was much too stringent, for Luke says nothing about this man's willingness to follow on such terms.

Now Jesus was not condemning sleeping quarters or funeral attendance or family relationships. What he was after was a man giving himself in absolute abandonment. These men counted the cost but were not willing to pay the price. It seems there was really only one reason why they did not respond to the lure of the heights. The venture was too demanding. After all, is not this our basic reason for not answering Christ's call? We really do not dare to do it.

James Denney was right. The Scotch saint used to say: "There is only one religious difficulty . . . the difficulty of being religious."

If we could only realize that when we "go," it is for his purpose and through his presence and in his power.

One of our quaint pioneer preachers used to read the words of Paul, "I can do all things," and declare to his

congregation that such was impossible. He would then
reach in his pocket, take some money out, and place it
on the pulpit, exclaiming he would bet that the man
from Tarsus was unable to keep his vow. Then he would
read the rest of the sentence ". . . through Christ which
strengtheneth me" (Phil. 4:13). Slowly, he would pick
up the money and return it conceding that Paul was right.
Surely it is only through the Christ who strengthens us
that we have the stamina to do all things.

We have a price to pay, but the Lord always gives us
the strength to make the payment.

Sometime ago I was seeking to lead a young adult to
the way eternal. I presented the good news to him as
best I could. When I concluded, he said, "Wallace, I
appreciate your interest in me, but the truth of the
matter is I am just not man enough to be a Christian."
I answered, "Jerry, neither am I man enough to be a
Christian, but Christ is Lord enough to make me a
Christian if I will let him."

This is why we have the strength to "go"—because we
have first come to him. That is the one reason why we
"can do all things."

II

Then, Jesus said, "Make disciples . . . baptizing . . . in
the name of the Father and of the Son and of the Holy
Spirit, teaching them . . . all that I have commanded
you." We have *a truth to tell*.

I think it is not being unfaithful to the text—I know

it is not betraying the content of the first tidings of the
church—to suggest that the heart of their message was
Christ. For though they worshiped the Father and witnessed in the power of the Spirit, their great good news
was the exaltation of the crucified Christ and living Lord.

We may quarrel a bit with Karl Barth concerning his
lack of emphasis on God and the Holy Spirit. One could
not say, however, that the place he gives to Jesus Christ
is anything but preeminent.

It may be a bit out of context, but increasingly I
appreciate some words of William Lyon Phelps. Yale's
great English professor who was an even greater Christian,
said, "I am a unitarian—I believe Christ is the only God!"

If you say to exalt Christ in this fashion is presump-
tuous, I agree. But can you ever presume upon an essential? If you say lifting Christ as our one hope is being
narrow-minded in the face of other creeds and faiths, I
would admit the guilt. But is it wrong to hold up the
truth? Could it not be that our temperate theology has
led us to timid tidings? Dare we show moderation when
our world hangs over hell every day and we have the
one remedy for its deliverance?

The first followers of our Lord were anything but
moderate as they sought to make disciples, baptize them,
and teach what they had been commanded. What did
they consider vital as they ministered "in the name of
the Son"?

First, they sought to proclaim the cross. If we witness
"in the name of the Son," the first name we must present

is *Savior*. What does this confidence mean? Whatever else it may include, it certainly means, to quote Edwin Lewis, "recognition of his power to forgive sin."[2] The burden is removed. The guilt is gone. We walk tall in his grace. One who had recently received this power of forgiveness, said to me, "How wonderful it is to be free at last."

Then, the disciples preached the empty tomb. If they proclaimed the crucified Christ as Savior, they also extolled the risen Redeemer as *Lord*. "Faith in Christ as Lord means a recognition of his right to the utter possession of the believer's life."[3]

So these men were possessed men—possessed by a truth so living and lifting and liberating that their enemies not only admitted "that they had been with Jesus" (Acts 4:13) but that they had "turned the world upside down" in his name (Acts 17:6). This truth that possessed was a Lord that lived. "Why are you reading about a dead man?" a cynic asked Roy Rogers, upon observing the New Testament in the hands of the cowboy star who is a sincere Christian. "I beg your pardon," Mr. Rogers answered. "But you are interrupting a conversation I am having with One who is very much alive."

III

Finally, Jesus said, "I will be with you." We have *a goal to gain*. Oh, I know what some will say at this point. We ought to do good for the sake of goodness without thought of compensation. And there is virtue in such a statement. Yet, remember our Lord did not hestitate to speak of rewards.

"Rejoice . . . because your names are written in heaven" (Luke 10:20).

"There is no man that hath left house . . . or lands, for my sake, and the gospel's, but he shall receive an hundredfold now in this time . . . and in the world to come eternal life" (Mark 10:29–30).

"When the Son of man shall come in his glory . . . shall the King say unto them on his right hand, Come, ye blessed of my Father, inherit the kingdom prepared for you' " (Matt. 25:31–34).

But the recompense we speak of now is greater than his gifts or his heaven. The supreme reward is not a prize he bequeaths; it is his presence he bestows. "I will be with you."

We all know how human ties can inspire. A little child had been injured many miles away from an infirmary. The ministering physician was not certain if she could endure the surgery without sedation. "I can stand anything," she whispered, "if my daddy holds my hand."

"I saw her shadow on the wall," a soldier wrote describing Florence Nightingale passing with her little lamp through the crowded hospitals of Scutari. "I saw her shadow on the wall and kissed it."[4]

"You have not made much out of all these years," said one Devon man who had stayed ashore and grown sleek and wealthy to another who had served in the fleet of Francis Drake. "No," said the other, "I've not made much. I've been cold, hungry, shipwrecked, desperately frightened often; but I've been with the greatest Captain who ever sailed the seas!"[5]

If a father or a nurse or an admiral could give such inspiration, how infinitely greater is the lifting power of the divine Christ! Yet, as we have been reminded, our Lord's promise to be with us is one that is conditional. "I will be with you," depends upon our going "in the name of the Son."

This then leads us to the second goal that is not definitely specified but is constantly implied. It is as we go in his name that his spirit works through us to lead others to the fellowship eternal.

They are out there . . . everywhere . . . sons and daughters of the Father, waiting for a brother to point them to him. This is how the early church was started. It is what will keep it redemptive now.

Years ago, I was preaching in a small country church in the hills of Virginia. I still remember how the caretaker of that little church prayed for his soldier son to become a Christian. The young man had just returned from overseas. One night, he came, and during the service, he felt the consuming persuasion of the Master. At the close, he came to the altar and was wonderfully converted. I knew then as I know now that it happened not because of the evangelist's preaching as much as the father's praying. I can still remember that old bell-ringing sexton, in the joy that knows no equal, saying over and over: "That's my boy! That's my boy!"

Will you and I say with all of our lives in the strength of his love: "That's my brother! That's my sister! That's my world!" and more, will we pay the price and tell the truth that we may gain the goal—the bringing home of the lost ones to the Father?

Notes

1. Elton Trueblood, *The Company of the Committed* (New York: Harper and Brothers, 1961), p. 37.

2. Edwin Lewis, *The Practice of the Christian Life* (Philadelphia: The Westminster Press, 1942), p. 11.

3. *Op.* cit., p. 11.

4. Alistair Maclean, *High Country* (London: Allenson and Co., 1934), p. 77.

5. James S. Stewart, *A Faith to Proclaim* (New York: Charles Scribner's Sons), p. 151.

3

The
Confident
Postscript

"Go . . . tell his disciples and Peter."

Mark 16:7

Whatever else this tremendous word of faith says to us, "Go tell his disciples and Peter," there is one thing that seems to tower above all else. Peter, who had promised so valiantly and fallen so wretchedly, was included so mercifully.

This text hooks and holds my heart with assurance and encouragement that few others bring. I make no apology for the personal element here. As I read this angelic word, it seems my name is substituted for Peter's. What hope this brings. Regardless of the promises I have broken, the vows I have neglected, the denials I have made, I am included in the sphere of his affection and in his commission to redeem the world. "And Peter"—"and me"—"and you."

Now why did Jesus send this hopeful message, this postscript of faith? I think there are at least four reasons.

I

In the first place, *Jesus still loved Peter.* "Where there is life, there is hope," is not always true. There may be a coma from which there is no restoration. There may be an indifferent heart that will simply not respond.

But where there is love there is hope. Where the eternal mercy of God flows like a mountain stream through the actions of his followers there is hope. Where the grace of a Calvary-led Savior works through simple deeds of unselfish kindness in the lives of his own, there is hope. Where the blessed Holy Spirit uses the child-like witness of a devoted disciple who is completely committed to redemptive love there is hope.

"Love never fails," said Paul. But, we say, the apostle was wrong. Love failed Judas. And literally millions of others, objects of sincere affection, have failed in their response and devotion to the outgoing love of those concerned. And the rich young ruler? Mark says that "Jesus beholding him loved him" but the evangelist also adds that he went away. Surely love failed.

No! No! The loved one failed, not the lover. Judas, love's object failed; not Jesus, love's subject. The love that comes to us from Christ and pours out to others never fails. Its desires may not be fulfilled. Its hopes may not be realized. Its dreams may not come true. But this love, if not received, can still be held and shared and the glory of its utter self-forgetfulness will be constantly lifting us ever closer to him who is love itself. No! love never fails because Christ never fails.

One said to a nurse attending a baby whose illness

was incurable, "You can do nothing for that child."
"Yes," answered the nurse, "I can love him." Who would
not have said: "It is too late for Peter—you can do nothing
for him. He has denied. He has disowned. He is a
failure." But Jesus loved him from disowner to disciple,
from reed to rock. At first our Lord called him away
from his fishing. Now he was calling him away from his
failing.

The nurse was right. We can love. "I can love him"
changed Peter from one who had denied with an oath
to one who witnessed with a passion.

It will work today. "I can love him" still turns gloom
into glory, despair into assurance, nothing into everything.

II

Not only did Jesus love Simon, but because of that
love and in the strength of that love, *Christ forgave him.*
Of course, Peter repented. We read after his denial that
he wept bitterly" (Matt. 26:75). It is doubtful if he ever
completely removed from his mind the memory of his
failure in the courtyard. At least we know how utterly
dependent on the Lord he was after this.

When the forgiveness of God pours over one's life,
always two things occur. First, there is new *surrender*
to the tasks that confront us. Second, there is the
strength given to us in their performance. For proof of
this, you have but to glance at those in the New Testament who experienced his pardon.

The very first thing that Matthew did after becoming
a follower was to give a great banquet in the Master's

honor. Nor did his enlistment to discipleship end there.
His life became a table where hungry men could come
and dine.

Out of the abundance of a freshly forgiven heart, Mary
broke the alabaster flask and anointed Jesus. Her life
became one of fragrant faith as she became Easter's herald
of hope.

Do you recall the story of the Philippian jailer? Following the orders of his superiors, he placed Paul and
Silas in the dungeon cell and locked their feet in stocks.
Both had been severely beaten, but he paid no attention
to the wounds that needed balm. Then you will remember
salvation came to his heart and home, and in the joy of
a forgiven and cleansed life he not only washed their
wounds but took the two men to his house and saw
that they were fed.

This was Simon's experience. The Master's cleansing
grace brought the renewal that rededication always brings.
Then came Pentecost, and for Peter a tremendous life
donation.

> Times without number have I prayed
>   "This only once forgive";
> Relapsing when Thy hand was stayed,
>   And suffered me to live.
>
> Yes now the kingdom of Thy peace,
>   Lord, to my heart restore;
> Forgive my vain repentances,
>   And bid me sin no more.

CHARLES WESLEY

Forgiveness brought surrender and strength to Peter. It will bring surrender and strength, or to use the synonyms of Charles Wesley, repentance and restoration to us.

III

Jesus loved Peter. He forgave Peter. *He still trusted Peter.*

This last statement may be the most amazing fact of all. Look at the spiritual collapse of Simon in the courtyard. If he had fallen apart so miserably under the pressure of a few antagonists, what would he do against the adversity of the Sanhedrin, to say nothing of Rome?

And yet, *"Go, tell his disciples and Peter!"* What could be more astounding, more encouraging, more thrilling than his invincible confidence of Christ?

"Thou art Simon," Jesus had said. "Thou shalt be called Cephas." That is, "you will be like rock." And when Jesus spoke these words, the Galilean fisherman was about as rocky as a foot of slush after the sun has melted the ice.

"I will build my church," Jesus proclaimed, "and the gates of hell shall not prevail against it." Following such a bold affirmation, Jesus explained that such discipleship involved a cross. His band of twelve had no earthly idea what he was talking about. Not only that, but their first ministry of mercy after these words, an attempt to heal an epileptic boy, was a complete washout.

"Be of good cheer," he declared, "I have overcome the world." And the next morning he hung from a bloody cross, his purpose rejected, his mission forsaken, his kingdom betrayed.

How deeply is my own heart stirred by this valiant confidence; this high expectancy of Christ!

Note also that this hope required three years before fulfilment. This was not a quick transition for Peter, nor was it an easy one. A serious operation often requires a deep incision. But always our Lord expected that the man of Pentecost would emerge.

Indeed, it is this holy optimism that has built the church. When the fellowship was young, had you and I been in Carthage, we should have seen a young man given over to the lusts of the earthy. If we had followed him to Rome and Milan we should have observed only a dissipated life. But Christ saw in Augustine the greatest spiritual power of the century.

Halfway between that day and our day, the thirteenth century viewed its generation as one that was morally bankrupt and the church and minister were little better. Had we been in a village of central Italy called Assisi, we should have seen only a youthful playboy absorbed in the wreckless frustrations of his age. But Christ saw in Saint Francis the man who would bring Europe beneath the shadow of the cross.

And one could go on and on. Christ saw in a young theologian of sixteenth-century Germany a man he needed to bring the reformation. But it was only when Christ led Luther from regulations without to redemption within that this purification was accomplished.

In much the same manner two hundred years later, our Lord took a brilliant young don from Oxford named Wesley. When law came out and love came in, Wesley straddled a horse and helped save England from a revolution.

This is the hour we were born to serve. His trust still is certain if we are yielded.

IV

The last point has already been anticipated. *Jesus still planned to use Peter.* He proposed to make him, in the power of the Spirit, commander of the church.

Follow this man now who once seemed so weak but in the fellowship of his risen Lord became so strong. Walk with him through the remainder of his experiences as they are recorded in the New Testament. The Master's confidence has been fulfilled. The rock has been formed. Watch him as the spokesman of the church, declaring with certainty at Pentecost that "this Jesus hath God raised up, whereof we all are witnesses" (Acts 2:32).

Listen as before the Jewish council Peter defends the faith in the name of Jesus Christ: "There is none other name under heaven given among men, whereby we must be saved" (Acts 4:12).

Why, you ask, is Christ able to use Peter in this fashion? Hear the words of a sermon he preached to the Christian Jews of Asia Minor: "You were indeed astray like sheep, but you have come back now to the Shepherd and Guardian of your souls." (Pet. 2:25, Moffatt).

This is the witness of Peter from his own experience.
This is the testimony of his own life. He leans in glad
confidence now not on himself but on the strength of his
crucified and risen Christ.

What about those of us who have hundreds of times
been negligent and indifferent, even cold? His grace he
still yearns to impart. His strength he still desires to
share. His presence he still longs to give.

But, you say, I have failed so often. And I. How
many opportunities I have wasted. How many chances I
have missed. Yet, "I am with you alway," is a fact upon
which we can lean our shaky souls and wavering witness.
This promise—no, it is more than that—this reality that
he is with us is able to give us dedication that knows no
denial. But let us remember it is only through him that
such certainty can be ours.

A week of spiritual renewal in our church was truly
one of the most rewarding experiences of my ministry.
Many marvelous surprises were in evidence and God
moved mightily upon the life of our fellowship.

As every pastor knows it is easier to go away for a
mission such as this than to conduct one's own services.
There are a number of reasons for this. For one thing,
no one is as close to his own as a minister and often this
makes preaching, especially preaching on local community
evils, difficult indeed. Another is that often the merit
of a new voice is far more acceptable. If a minister has
labored in the same parish for two or more years, the
craft of preparing new sermons is not an easy one.

Our week of renewal was conducted during Holy Week and this is not an easy time. I must confess that by Thursday evening as minister and congregation prepared for the Gethsemane hour of our Lord, my heart was quite heavy. My secretary anticipating the burden she knew I felt, left a note on my desk for me to read before entering the pulpit. Here is what it said: "Oh yes you can . . . for the Lord is your strength."

God did use me that night. And what a miracle he made of the fisherman from Galilee as he used him in initiating a worldwide witness.

He will use you if you will let him!

4

The Greatest Question

"When they had dined, Jesus saith to Simon Peter, Simon, son of Jonas, lovest thou me more than these?"

John 21:15

Our Lord made it a habit to teach by asking questions. The Pharisees who seemed so stubbornly hostile to his messianic credentials were asked, "What think ye of Christ?" (Matt. 22:42).

To those who would have made community a matter of space to travel instead of concern to share, he told the story that we refer to as the parable of the good Samaritan, concluding with the query, "Which of these . . . was neighbour?" (Luke 10:36).

And when many were forsaking because the road of discipleship appeared to be not a path of pleasure but a trail of thorns, he inquired of the twelve, "Will ye also go away?" (John 6:67).

But the question Jesus asked by the Sea of Galilee early one morning after his resurrection was the greatest question. Indeed, what we think *of* him—what we do *for* him—how close we stay *to* him depends upon our answer to this question Jesus asked Simon.

Earlier the Lord appeared to Thomas for faith's sake.
Here he appears to Peter for love's sake.

I

Note first *the object of love.* "Lovest thou me?" Jesus
asked. This must always be first. He did not ask if Simon
loved the sheep. This is necessary, but our regard for the
sheep depends upon our relationship to the Shepherd.

Peter had disowned his Lord in the courtyard. Peter
had forsaken him at Calvary. Yet, though cowardice had
come in, Peter's love for the Master had not gone out.
True, Peter had indicated little evidence of its presence,
but the time would be soon when this love for the Christ
fortified by the assurance of the Spirit would change him
from coward of the distant followers to captain of the
church militant.

The Holy Spirit does not simply come to believing
minds. He comes to loving hearts. Peter had to declare
himself before he could receive the inner presence. Peter
had to affirm his stand before he could proclaim a joyful
message.

Note that Jesus did not ask Simon if he loved to feed
the sheep. In just a moment he would commission him
with this great task of sharing his witness, but the initial
question was, "Lovest thou me?" As a minister of the
gospel of Christ, I must beware lest my office become a
profession instead of a calling. Certainly I must prepare
my sermons and give constant attention to the communica-
tive elements involved in preaching. But when the

substance of the sermon takes precedence over the gladness of the gospel, my effectiveness as an ambassador for the King will be very limited indeed.

It is an old story—that of the young man who delivered his first sermon in the presence of his preacher-father—but the lesson involved is constantly needed. He had labored diligently on the sermon and, he thought, delivered it satisfactorily. But his father made no comment as they returned home from the service. Neither did he commit himself the entire day. Finally, as they drove to the train station the following morning, the son decided he would question his father. "I simply can't return to college, Dad," he said, "until you tell me how you think I made out yesterday." "Son," the elderly man replied, "some men stand in front of the cross when they preach and others stand behind it." He made his point and the youthful disciple never forgot it.

Now, where do you and I stand, not initially in regard to the sheep but in regard to the Savior? Where do we stand, not primarily with respect to the delivery of our tidings but the dedications of our lives? Do we love him?

II

Observe, in the second place, *the demand of love:* "more than these." To what does "these" refer?

Jesus and the disciples had just finished breakfast. Could the Master have directed Peter's gaze at the spot where the meal had been completed, thus asking concerning the food? If he did, then "more than these" means more than *material things.*

Our Lord never meant for one of his children to go hungry. You will recall in the Sermon on the Mount, he said: "Take no thought, saying, What shall we eat? . . . Seek ye first the kingdom." (Matt. 6:31,33) But he did not intend that we seek the Kingdom on empty stomachs. He merely wanted us to put his cause first and not to be tied to that which was of secondary importance.

This same principle applies to the demand he made of one whom we call the rich young ruler. "Go, sell whatsoever thou hast, and give to the poor," Jesus said to the young ruler. Jesus did not say it was wrong to have things. He did feel it was wrong to keep them to yourself while your brothers starved about you.

Jesus may have pointed to the nets during this conversation with Peter. If he did, then "more than these" means more than *temporal tasks.* It may very well be that Jesus was reiterating here his initial summons to Simon; he wanted him to be catching something more important than fish.

Make no mistake about it—this is the supreme assignment of those who belong to the body of Christ. Winning people to him is not the only business of the church, but it is the main business of the church. Regardless of how we may be succeeding in other areas, if we fail here we are failing our Lord and our primary purpose for existence.

These remarks are not addressed only to those in church

vocations. It has been said in similar ways quite often, but I like the cogent phrasing of a friend of mine—an outstanding dentist who is a glowing witness for his Lord. He said, "I pull teeth to pay my expenses—my occupation is soul-winning." Regardless of one's employment, the task is temporal if it only includes catching fish. It becomes eternal when in addition we begin enlisting men.

Or the Master may have nodded toward the rest of the disciples when he asked Simon this question. If he did, then "more than these" means more than the *other followers*. Jesus did not mean "Do you love me more than *you* love them?" as he may have intended in regard to food and nets. He meant, "Do you love me more than *they* love me?" If this were the case, there are those who suggest that Jesus should not have put Peter's love on a competitive basis. However, Peter was the one who had revealed so much promise. It was he who had declared with amazing spiritual insight, "Thou art the Christ" (Matt. 16:16). And it was he who had professed heroically, "I will lay down my life for thy sake" (John 13:37). Yes, and it was this impulsive fisherman and denying apostle that Jesus had chosen to become the leader of the church. His love, especially for that hour, had to go further—had to go deeper—than the love of the others.

Our Lord had earlier asked a group of potential followers, "What do ye more than others?" (Matt. 5:47). It was a query that most assuredly implied competition. So perhaps here Jesus is in reality asking Peter, "How much stronger is your love than the others?"

III

Finally, let us look at *the task of love:* "Feed my lambs."
This is what we do when we love Christ. This is what
we do when we love him more than all else. How many
hungry sheep, how many starving lambs are looking to
us for refreshment of faith and nourishment of love? God
grant that those of us in the fellowship of the church
shall see that this is imperative. In John's Gospel, this
is our Lord's first command after his resurrection. It is
a command that has lost none of its urgency or fervency
in our day.

The great task of those of us who belong to the body
of Christ is not to raise the budget but to feed the lambs.
This is true for minister and laymen alike. The laity of
our church are not called to be pew-sitters but sheep-
feeders. My initial summons from the Master as his
minister is not to supervise a program or call a meeting
or operate a mimeograph. Our Lord's first command to
the captain of the church that day by the Sea of Galilee
was not to organize a committee—it was to feed the lambs.
This is my commission and it is yours. How can it be done?

In two ways, I think. First, we can feed the lambs by
devoted living. Seeing a saint is better than hearing a
sermon. A saint in the New Testament was not a patriarch
with a long beard. It was simply a disciple with a glowing
experience. William James was right when he said that
our religion is either "a dull habit or an acute fever."
We read in Acts concerning two that maintained a torrid
temperature: "When they saw (not heard) the boldness

of Peter and John, . . . they took knowledge of them, that
they had been with Jesus" (Acts 4:13).

I was preaching in one of our Southern cities when an
elderly minister came and sat on the front pew. He was
deaf and could catch but little of the service, yet his
presence was an inspiration to me. I had known him in
years gone by and both loved and respected him deeply.
His comment after the service was of great significance
to me. "Wallace," he said with not little emotion, "you
certainly looked a good sermon today."

Was it Bishop Quayle who said, "It is more important
to be a sermon than hear a sermon?" I fear that my
old preacher friend was wrong about me, but in deepest
humility since then I have asked God to help me justify
his compliment.

We can feed the lambs by heroic witnessing. In just
a few days Peter would declare the gospel with such power
at Pentecost that three thousand sheep would be fed.
The other disciples joined him in a witness crusade that
has extended to the present hour. Certainly it cost them
their lives but safety seemed to be their last concern.
Listen to what one of their preachers said: "I do not
account my life of any value nor as precious to myself,
if only I may accomplish my course and the ministry
which I received from the Lord Jesus, to testify to the
gospel of the grace of God" (Acts 20:24, RSV).

Some know today what it means to be persecuted for
righteousness' sake. I am thinking of one who was my
roommate and dear friend during seminary days. In the

deep South he held high the gospel banner professing that it was for all men. What cross-burners could not do to him, prejudiced minds tried. But his critics could not soften him. The Klan could not scare him. Transferring him could not silence him. He has paid in terms of "promotion" (a word I detest) but what strength his witness has brought to others!

Persecution, I think, for most of us at least in this country, will be a frown, or a snub, or a jeer, or a "demotion." But even if we be wounded for others' transgressions and bruised for others' iniquities, are we not right in affirming with one who knew the the meaning of sacrifice, that it is better to have scars on the body than scars on the soul?

And won't we be in good company?

There was Peter who fed the lambs and died for it in Rome. There was Stephen who gave his witness and died for it in Jerusalem. There was Polycarp who exalted Christ and died for it in Smyrna. There Savonarola who fed the lambs and died for it in Florence. There was Latimer who declared his faith and died for it in Oxford. There was Jim Elliott and Paul Carlson and Burleigh Law—all modern disciples—all present-day saints who fed the lambs and died on foreign fields. There were others who have suffered and died on native soil. And above all, there was Jesus Christ who gave his witness and died at Calvary.

The greatest days of persecution are still the greatest days of Kingdom building and spiritual growth. Now—everywhere there are lambs to feed. God grant that we have the food to share.

5

The Neglected Joy

"But Thomas, one of the twelve, . . . was not with them when Jesus came."

John 20:24

Thomas was not with them when Jesus came. There is an overtone of tragedy in that sentence. Oh, I know he came later. He came as the German boy who volunteered for our American army during World War I came. The recruiting officer, somewhat surprised, asked, "But do you wish to fight against your former people?" His answer was: "When I came to America, I came all."

Thomas would soon do that, committing his all to Christ, he would spend the rest of his life revealing his love to others. But when our Lord first appeared to the disciples, Thomas was not present.

The voice of the Lord came to the young Isaiah in the temple at Jerusalem, saying, "Whom shall I send, and who will go for us?" Listen to his answer for it is vital. "Here am I: send me" (Isa. 6:8) Although it is important to be sent, it is more important to be here, to be available when the call of need comes. The men and women who have influenced my life the most have not been the noisy shouters or the loud pray-ers. It has been those who were simply present when they were needed. What we do in regard to our commission depends upon where we are in regard to our call. Our assignment for Christ is determined by our attendance upon Christ.

For many of us, this is really not a matter that is important. We laughingly say:

> In the world's broad field of battle,
> In the bivouac of life,
> There you will find a Christian soldier
> Represented by his wife.

But remember that there is a very good chance if you are not at your station, listening to your summons, receiving his guidance for your service, that the bit of the Kingdom God wants to build through you may never be established.

How much we lack when we are not present in the fellowship of those who serve the risen Lord. How much Thomas lost by not being with his fellow disciples when Jesus came.

What did he miss? What do we miss?

I

First, Thomas missed *the Lord's presence.* The disciples met to rejoice in Christ's triumph over the grave. The living Lord came and stood in their presence in risen reality, but Thomas was not there to see him.

Now there is nothing we need today so desperately as those who are constantly conscious of the reality of Christ as he meets with us to sustain and strengthen and send us out.

I do not intend to suggest that the Christian life is all ecstacy. Perhaps this was Simon's mistake on the mount of transfiguration. It was a grand hour for the bold fisherman as well as for his associates. For a brief period they were co-sharers in the companionship of Calvary. Peter announced to Jesus, "Master, it is good for us to be here." What he meant was, "It would be good for us to stay here."

But consecration on the mountain, if it is genuine, must point to courage in the valley. All too soon Peter would lose heart and even deny knowing his Lord. Jesus did not intend that Simon stay on the mountain. He had intended that Simon stay with the Master who had been with him on the mountain.

Now the purpose of the coming of the Holy Spirit lies just at this point. How could the faith of the disciples become potent? How could their ministry become powerful? Only as they had a permanent awareness of his presence. Thus the significance of Pentecost: the Christ who had been *with* them for three years was not *in* them forever.

But, of course, Christ could not have come in the Spirit had he not risen from the tomb. It was this risen reality that Thomas missed. And it is everything!

I have some good friends who believe Christ's high ideals could not be buried, that his pure motives arose, and that his ethical standards overcame death. They do not hold, however, to the fact that our Lord, himself, walked victoriously from the grave. How much we miss when we do not have his living fellowship in our hearts to give a living faith to our lives!

II

Thomas missed *the Lord's proof.*

According to the Fourth Gospel, the first time that Jesus appeared to the disciples in a group was the very time that Thomas was absent. The first thing the Lord did after greeting them was to show them his hands and his side. This was the thing that Thomas had put down as his requirement for believing. The proof he demanded was the proof he missed on Christ's first visit.

The disciples' first response to the resurrection was not one of joy. "Nonsense," Luke informs us. And again the beloved physician, as Paul describes him, says, "They shrank back in terror" (Luke 24:37, Phillips).

Yet we read in the Gospel of John that immediately after our Lord showed the disciples his hands and his side they were glad. There could not be any doubt now. John had seen him die. Mary Magdalene had also been at Calvary. She, too, had given witness that he lived. He still had upon his body the marks that caused his death. But he was alive! It is important to note that this was not just some vague spiritual specter that they encountered. An apparition would hardly have invited Thomas to not just see and believe but touch and know.

For the benefit of those who disbelieve the physical

resurrection, it is more difficult for me to believe that
Jesus Christ would have requested Thomas to do something had it been impossible to do it. And when one
gets right down to it, there are not many ghosts who can
cook a meal (John 21:9) or break a loaf (Luke 24:30)
or eat a fish (Luke 24:42-43).

Sometimes the way of faith excels the way of reason.
To be sure Jesus invited Thomas to come by reason. He
said: "Because thou hast seen me, thou hast believed."
But he added, "Blessed are they that have not seen, and
yet have believed." It would seem that this received his
greater emphasis.

III

Thomas missed *the Lord's peace.* "Jesus came and stood
among them and said to them, "Peace be with you" (John
20:19, RSV).

This was a friendly greeting but it was infinitely more.
It was a spiritual benediction. True, two of them had
seen the empty tomb. True, they had all heard Mary's
affirmation. But they had not seen for themselves. Then
he came in visible reality with his gift of peace.

The Lord's blessing was of great help to them for two
reasons. First, they were anything but certain that he
was actually alive. I doubt seriously if I know anything
more pathetic than a morally decent person, even a church
member, who will not trust his soul to the glad news of
the resurrection. And, of course, it affects as nothing else
one's service for the cause of Christ.

I am thinking of one, who until recently, was making little contribution to the kingdom. Now there is a glow on her face, a concern for her neighbors in her heart, and a daily joy in her witness. When questioned about the change in her life, she answered: " 'He rose from the dead,' is no longer a formula. It is a fact."

The peace Christ gave was of vast importance, in the second place, because the disciples' own dreams had perished at Calvary. It is not going too far to say that when he came alive, they came alive.

Notice that Jesus presented his peace to the disciples in this particular scene not once but twice. "Peace be unto you," he said and showed them his hands and his side. And again, "Peace be unto you," then added, "as my Father hath sent me, even so send I you." Do you see what this means? The first time that he offered peace he revealed the scars of his sacrifice; they had to have the confidence to know. The second time that he offered peace he revealed the duty of discipleship; they had to have the summons to share. Confidence and commission. Assurance and activity. Trust and task.

Our Lord knew what had to come first, for there can never be purpose in the world until there is peace in the heart. For eight days Thomas walked in misery, and yet there are those who spend an entire lifetime in despair.

IV

Thomas missed *the Lord's passion.*
This is the final point and it is a perfectly natural

transition. Really, we fully anticipated it as we concluded the preceding paragraph. He revealed himself to them. He showed the marks of Calvary. He gave them peace. He said as John relates and as we suggested, "as my Father has sent me, even so send I you." Then he breathed on them, and said, "Receive ye the Holy Ghost." Thus it is that as our Lord lives within, we have the desire to witness without.

For more than a week Thomas lost the experience of witnessing to his risen Redeemer. We never become transmitters of the resurrection truth until this tremendous reality overwhelms us.

"We trusted that it had been he which should have redeemed Israel," one of his followers said. Then Jesus broke bread and Cleopas recognized him. So what? He immediately went out to tell.

How many of us let our faith stop short of the empty tomb. Like Cleopas, our hope becomes a past experience, a wistfulness that only looks back. But when we know the Lord who lives, the lights shine in our hearts and the fires flame in our souls giving us the passion of triumphant witness.

Nels Ferre is right when he says: "We can have a new world at the price only of a newfound faith in the reality of the resurrection."

Thomas and his brother-disciples, assured of the grave-conquering Christ, redeemed their world. The living Lord will give us the passion and the power to redeem ours.

Away with gloom, away with doubt!
With all the morning stars we sing;
With all the sons of God we shout
The praises of a King.

When he lives in the heart, we must tell it to the world.

6

The
Victorious
Journey

"While they were talking . . . Jesus himself drew near
and went with them."

Luke 24:15, RSV

It is amazing what a trip with Jesus Christ will do. Here are two travelers who leave Jerusalem in the "slough of despond" and before they have long arrived in Emmaus are on the highroad of certainty.

Listen to them soon after departing on their journey: "We had hoped that he was the one to redeem Israel" (Luke 24:21, RSV). Now, hear one speak to the other as a result of sharing walk and welcome with Jesus: "Weren't our hearts glowing while he was with us?" (Luke 24:32, Phillips).

Something happened during those few hours that changed their futility into faith and that turned their anguish into assurance. To be sure the truth is that these dejected disciples encountered their living Lord. But what was involved in this companionship that brought to them such confidence?

I

First, *Scripture was interpreted.* "Beginning with Moses and all the prophets," Luke informs us, "he interpreted to them in all the scriptures the things concerning himself" (Luke 24:27, RSV). This is the most that a shepherd can do for his flock. It is the least he can do and still be a faithful minister of Jesus Christ.

The fellowship that afternoon on the Emmaus Road was a *scriptural* approach to certainty. It was our Lord's first step in his effort to reveal himself to them. Now to me this is significant. It says that it is the method by which we, too, must reveal the Redeemer, must prove his presence. Why is it that we are not more effective interpreters?

I think the initial answer is simply that we do not *read* the Scriptures. Dr. Edwin Mims, that grand old patriarch of English literature, used to say, "The Bible gathers more dust on ministerial shelves than any other book." Perhaps he would have included layman's libraries as well.

"I do not read the Bible anymore," said a certain layman I know. "Parts of it I once read seemed like fairy stories and I felt intellectually cheated."

His statement was as frightening as it was immature. How different are the words of the giant souls. Karl Barth said, "I read the Bible like a ship-wrecked man." Soren Kierkegaard said, "The Bible is God's personal love letter to me."

The second answer, and this may sound severe, has to

be that we do not *believe* the Scriptures. Do you recall our Lord's words of rebuke to his traveling companions that day on the highway? "O foolish men," he said, ". . . slow of heart to believe all that the prophets have spoken!"

This is the very purpose of his word—to guide us to faith. Writing of his resurrection appearances, John says, "these are written that you may believe."

Great truths—his coming, his living, his dying, his rising —all wait for the door of our faith to open and admit their radiance.

The final point is we do not *preach* the Scriptures. To be sure we always read some portion of his Word from the pulpit or behind the lectern in our church school room. This is customary. This is proper. This is expected. But where do we go from there?

How often we have read some great sentences of faith— some lifting thoughts from the Old or New Covenants —and then proceeded to give a review of current events. Or we have based the theme on some popular novel or religious periodical or personal happening. These sources are all right for added attractions but not as origins for development of a sermon, as foundations for preaching.

"Thy Word is a lamp unto my feet, and a light unto my path" (Ps. 119:105).

This is the genesis for our message.

I rather doubt if a certain layman complimented his minister with some terse words at the conclusion of a morning service. He said, "Preacher, if that text had been infected with smallpox, the sermon never would have caught it." How great is the need to preach the Scriptures.

Paul was right. The gospel is the power of God for salvation. It must be expounded and explained with confidence and clarity.

In his excellent book, *Proclaiming the Word,* Ronald Sleeth says "Christian preaching is primarily biblical preaching. For only as we faithfully interpret the Bible can we be aware of God's Word to us, for that is where he speaks to his faithful."[1]

II

Bread was broken. "As he sat at meat with them, he took bread, and blessed it and brake, and gave to them" (Luke 24:30). Not only was the avenue to assurance scriptural; it was *sacramental.*

If you want to know how important this approach to God is, read again the words of those who shared this supper. "They told . . . how he was known of them in breaking of bread" (Luke 24:35).

I am not sure what this experience says to our fast, fuming, frustrated century. But it says to me that Christ has the reality and the radiance to turn a secular happening into a sacred hour. Dr. Trueblood has it in a succinct sentence. "The table is really the family altar!"[2]

The supper room at Emmaus can be just as meaningful as the upper room in Jerusalem. With his presence to bless, a common moment becomes a ceremonial meal. With his love to transform, every supper becomes a sacrament. This fact could change our lives if we would believe it and appropriate its truth as an extension of the kingdom.

Of course, it was a holy hour when our Lord shared the last supper with his disciples. I can but express my opinion when I say that the greatest service of worship in the Christian church is when we follow their example by partaking and celebrating this blessed communion. Jesus took a cup and after giving thanks to the Father, he gave it to the disciples and said, "Drink ye all of it; for this is my blood of the new testament, which is shed for many for the remission of sins" (Matt. 26:27–28).

And yet, it was the same Lord that said, "For whosoever shall give you a cup of water to drink in my name, because ye belong to Christ, verily I say unto you, he shall not lose his reward" (Mark 9:41).

Jesus gave the wine: this says he is our Deliverer. We give water: this says we are his disciples. It is not the content of the glass; it is the consecration of the giver that is vital.

Let me illustrate this with an example that moved me deeply though I cannot recall where I heard it. Some war-weary soldiers, just back from the front lines, were resting and having a bit of refreshment after narrowly escaping death. The temporary canteen behind the battlefield was supplied by a young woman whose duty was simply serving sandwiches and hot coffee. I cannot remember whether it was the chaplain or another officer who made the suggestion that prayer be lifted before the meal's

completion. But I can never forget the words of one of
the infantrymen. He said, "Is that necessary, sir?" Then
pointing toward the one who was serving them, he said,
"She has been pouring Christ into every cup."

Paul speaks of the power of Christ that enables us to
sit in heavenly places. Is not the common place a heavenly
place when the Master is there? He was not known to
them in the liturgy of worship nor in the sound of anthem
nor in the proclamation of sermon, but in the breaking
of bread.

III

Hearts were warmed. As the disciples reflected upon the
radiant encounter, they said, "Did not our heart burn
within us, while he talked with us by the way, and while
he opened to us the scriptures?" (Luke 24:32). This
fellowship that lifted was not only scriptural and sacramental. It was *spiritual*.

All these experiences are possible because of one supreme event: *Christ had risen*. A living Lord interpreted
the Word. A risen Savior divided the loaf. An eternal
Christ blessed the soul.

A ghost cannot explain Scriptures; a specter cannot
break bread; a phantom cannot warm hearts!

Make no mistake about it, these two followers of Jesus
who went from Jerusalem to Emmaus were different from
the two who a few hours later journeyed from Emmaus
to Jerusalem. This is the power of the good news: it
utterly changes—it divinely transforms.

I don't care how many Isaiahs you think there were. Perhaps there were a half-dozen. The thrilling thing is the transformation of the one who went into the Temple in utter despair and came out in the power of God to deliver Jerusalem.

So with these two disciples of Emmaus. Their grim despondency was turned into glad discovery. Their complete dejection became joyful certainty. Read again Luke's words: "They rose up the same hour, and returned to Jerusalem." And what was the news they brought? It was that Jesus had risen.

The Spirit of the living Christ still turns the darkness of despair into the dawn of day. At this very moment he is seeking to transform our highway of hopelessness into an expectant Emmaus and a joyful Jerusalem.

Listen to one who for over fifty magnificent years walked in radiant assurance with a living companion. His travels are over. His tidings have ceased. His task is done. What is it Wesley is saying? "The best of all is, God is with us!" Hear it again; not "has been," not "will be," *is!* That is not a dirge of depression. It is a hymn of hope. But more, it is a testimony of triumph. "Alleluia: for the Lord God omnipotent reigneth" (Rev. 19:6).

NOTES

1. Ronald Sleeth, *Proclaiming the Word* (New York: Abingdon Press, 1964).

2. Elton Trueblood, *The Common Ventures of Life* (New York: Harper, 1949), p. 76.

7

The Underrated Virtue

"But tarry ye in the city of Jerusalm, until ye
be endued with power from on high."

Luke 24:49

Our Lord's command to "Go make disciples" was dependent upon his instruction to "tarry in the city."

Most earnest Christians would admit the appeal of the constraint of Christ—the compelling urgency to act. We find much less fascinating the restraint of Christ—the necessary admonition to wait.

We sing:

> Lead on, O King Eternal,
>   The day of march has come;
> Henceforth in fields of conquest
>   Thy tents shall be our home:
> Through days of preparation
>   Thy grace has made us strong,
> And now, O King Eternal,
>   We lift our battle song.

And so we should.

But here is another hymn. It is not as popular but it is just as essential.

Not so in haste, my heart!
Have faith in God and wait;
Although He linger long,
He never comes too late.

In the light of Pentecost what is significant concerning this underrated virtue of waiting?

I

Why were the disciples to wait? And why were they commanded to wait in Jerusalem?

First, the disciples were commanded by the Lord to wait in Jerusalem because they needed to know the disciplined heart. It was essential that they realize the importance of obedience. This is something each of us must learn as followers of the faith. It is the doorway into the life abundant. "I was not disobedient unto the heavenly vision," declared Paul.

Second, obedience is the way for one to continue in the faith.

As late as Gethsemane our Lord found that obedience was the only way to serve his father and fulfil his mission.

The disciples had to realize the virtue of patient obedience before they could know the reward of devoted service.

So this rather prosaic period of waiting was incumbent upon the disciples, but it was not a stagnant repose. It was a disciplined duty. They were changing from disciples into apostles as they tarried.

When Dietrich Bonhoeffer was holding high the banner

during the war years in Germany, he even organized a small seminary. His emphasis here as all through his ministry was giving Christ the preeminent place in one's life . . . even in opposition to the Third Reich. Some of his students felt that if they stood against Hitler they would give up opportunities to serve the state churches, thus forfeiting the chance to preach sermons to the people. Listen to Bonhoeffer's answer: "One act of obedience is better than a hundred sermons."[1]

Then the disciples waited in Jerusalem because this was where the cross had been experienced. So you have to start here. Away with any belief or theology that attempts to begin anywhere else. Later it would be where they would start in their preaching, but now it was where they began in their allegiance.

The followers of Christ were not yet closely knit disciples. They would soon have the miraculous power of the Holy Spirit in their lives. However, they needed not only a great miracle to send them out but also a great memory to hold them up. This, you know, is one of the great purposes of the Eucharist. We receive the cup to remember the cross.

Whatever else the reasons for beginning the Christian witness in Jerusalem, one of them has to be that this was where the Lord suffered and died. It is always true that only when we begin at Calvary do we start at the place of supreme significance.

Of course, some will not like this emphasis. It made Peter mad the first time our Lord outlined his own

messianic mission which included crucifixion. But Jesus'
answer was "Get thee behind me, Satan: for thou savourest
not the things that be of God but the things that be of
man" (Mark 8:33). What he meant was that a cross-less
religion was a devilish one.

Finally, the disciples waited in Jerusalem because his
potential followers of the future were here. This group
was the nucleus of the church. Jesus said, "Ye shall be
witnesses . . . in *Jerusalem*, and in all Judaea, and in
Samaria and unto the uttermost part of the earth" (Acts
1:8).

But first he told them that "they should not depart
from Jerusalem" (Acts 1:4). Of course, we say today we
must go where the people are. What we often forget is
that we are leaving a particular element behind. Very
often that element is the lower-class group and we forget
that it was the common people, the masses, which often
make up the lower class, that our Lord came to seek and
to save. This is a crisis for the brotherhood, and it is also
a marvelous doorway of opportunity for the church.

Christianity became a world-wide witness, but it never
would had it not had the power to redeem at its front
door. If the Holy Spirit through these first devoted followers had not been able to transform Jerusalem, few
inroads could have been made across the Roman Empire.

This new faith would never have secured the merit of
"having favour with all the people," as Luke reminds us,
if they had not seen vital and victorious religion in the
lives of the disciples. Thus commanding the respect at

home, of *all the people* they felt in his power they were adequate to share the faith will *all the world.*

So often we do not start at Jerusalem; at home. Think of the poor we never see, the despised we never meet; the ragged we never know. We must not talk about going to the end of the earth when we do not even see the beginning of our parish. This is not just silky suburia—it may well be a filthy field that is dying for Christ's cultivation. "Who is my neighbor?" is not a question of geography but of grace.

II

Since the disciples were to practice patience in Jerusalem, how were they to wait?

In the first place, they were to wait *collectively*; they waited together. They were fearful. They were not certain as to all that the future included. They were as yet unlearned in the power of witness but they were together; "with one accord" says Luke.

> We are not divided,
> All one body we,
> One in hope and doctrine,
> One in charity.

Would to God that this were true today! Oh, the power of the church if we all were firmly united as the body of Christ!

I am often amazed at the petty differences we have. I remember once preaching in a church where friction had almost completely split the church. One group said that an organ was essential and the other side said that a piano was the only instrument for church use. You do not have to guess as to whether this church was a significant factor for good in community life.

These men were of varying temperaments. Peter was impulsive. Andrew was thoughtful. Thomas was suspicious. Philip was retiring. But they were waiting for that which would bring mighty union and in anticipation of this promised blessing, they were even now coming together.

Then they waited *prayerfully*. They continued, we are told, "in prayer and supplication." This was not time lost from a world crusade. Prayer is always the prelude to power. Hours spent in the closet of the quiet heart are never wasted.

Do you recall our Lord's words to the anxious and troubled Martha? "One thing is needful," he said, "Mary hath chosen that good part." There must be both: the sitting Mary and the serving Martha. But the secret of the patient heart is to wait at the Lord's feet before we rise on our own.

Moses led the children of Israel into the land of promise, but first he stayed alone with God in Midian. Jesus was able to inaugurate a kingdom only after forty days of patience and preparation in the desert. Paul helped make Christianity a world faith with his devoted witness, but first came the days of holy hush in Arabia.

The last thing is this—they waited *expectantly*. They knew that because of the resurrection anything was possible. And the Lord had promised the coming Comforter.

Dr. Gossip, that great Scotch preacher, felt that the people with expectant hearts were the ones who moved the world. "Always standing on tiptoe," was his phrase, "sure that something big may happen at any time."

Jesus had said, "Ye shall be baptized with the Holy Ghost not many days hence" (Acts 1:5). Something big was about to happen, and so they waited with eager outlook, confident that their Master's promise would come true.

III

What happened as a result of practicing this underrated virtue of patience? What occurred because they waited? The answer is, of course, the Holy Spirit came upon them. This resulted in two things.

First, they now had love for all men. I am not sure of all that Spirit baptism includes but I know it means this: God's love so fills our hearts that every needy life comes within the range of our affection.

Listen to the premium Jesus placed on such concern: "By this shall all men know that ye are my disciples, if ye have love one to another" (John 13:35). That is, the one great way we can prove our identity with the Savior is by sharing his regard for all our brothers.

I doubt if one can be paid a greater compliment than the words of tribute L. P. Jacks gave to Dick Sheppard. "Were all other proofs to fail us, a life such as his would be enough to justify us in saying that God is, and that

God is love."[2]

Then not only did they love all men but they had the power to witness of their faith to all men. The different New Testament translators have varied names for the Holy Spirit. He is called the Comforter, the Counselor, our Advocate, and the Divine Helper. But one word is invariably used when these writers describe what the Holy Spirit will do for Christ's followers. "Ye shall receive *power*," said Jesus (Acts 1:8).

The power of the Spirit is simply the truth of Christ. Jesus had said, "Ye shall know the truth and the truth shall make you free" (John 8:32), and he had also referred to the Holy Spirit as the "Spirit of truth." Thus knowing him led to declaring him.

An outstanding layman in our church recently shared with me an experience that I have been unable to forget. I requested that he write it down in the first person. To me it speaks of this essential which we are attempting to stress at this point.

"At the last fueling stop before flying over the 'hump' into China, our flight crews were briefed as to weather, enemy attacks, and navigational aids that were available to them. However, as soon as some of the crews completed a few raids, they often became indifferent concerning their briefings. As a result, every week there was continual loss of life as well as the loss of planes. This was needless and uncalled for.

"After the commanding officer had exercised every resort and technique to gain the attention of the crews and convince them of the great necessity of knowing their mission, he placed a sign over the entrance to the flight tent. This was the sign: 'What you don't know won't hurt you—it will kill you.' "

It is the knowledge of his love and the power of his presence that makes the church redemptive and will inevitably redeem the world.

But remember, we can never triumph in the world until we "tarry in the city."

NOTES

1. *Prophetic Voices in Contemporary Theology* (Nashville: Abingdon Press, 1966), p. 172.

2. *Dick Sheppard, Man of Peace* (London: James Clark and Co.).

8

The
Valiant
Vanguard

"Behold, he goeth before you into Galilee; there
shall ye see him."

Matthew 28:7

This is a significant word the angel of the empty tomb shared with the two Marys. It incorporates two great truths. First, the Lord went before them. Secondly, a bit later the Lord was with them.

Christ must be our vanguard. There are Galilees he must face and meet first. The writer of Proverbs said, "Trust in the Lord with all thine heart . . . and he shall direct thy paths (Prov. 3:5–6). It is a fitting description of our forward-going Lord.

Directing our course is the theme of the twenty-third Psalm, "He leadeth me." The shepherd had to go before the sheep because there were noxious plants and poisonous snakes and vicious animals.

The way I face today may not be easy, but by his going before I can be:

> Content, whatever lot I see,
> Since 'tis my God that leadeth me.

Then, as we suggested, not long after the angelic word

had been given to the women, the Lord was with them.
The point is, of course, that though there are times when
he must needs go before, he is never far away. The question of his presence is never in doubt.

The twenty-third Psalm does say, "He leadeth me."
But it also says, "Thou art with me."

Keeping these two thoughts together—that of his fore-
running and his fellowship—let us seek to follow this idea.

I

Christ goes before to guide us. This in a very real
sense is the purpose of the incarnation. Christ came to
live the way a man ought to live. He knows our tempta-
tions. He understands our tendency to yield to the lower
voices. In Gethsemane he tasted for all men the bitter
fruit; the heartache of doubt as to which road to walk.
This is often my difficulty and it is yours. He settled it,
and he went to his Calvary with confidence in the Father.
So may we.

Or grief has come to your heart. Tragedy has pierced
your soul and you feel that life no longer has meaning.
Jesus stood by a grave in Bethany. He was idolized by
many at first, yet surrounded by few at the end. The
home of Lazarus served often as his spiritual retreat. The
loss of his friend broke his heart.

When those closest to him walked no longer with him,
what a sensation of despondency and grief must have
welled up within him. Yet, "I am not alone," he affirmed
and walked with faith aflame to Golgotha.

One wants a guide who understands the road; one who knows the precipices, is aware of the pitfalls, and sees all the dangers. You can trust his leading. For though he faced the crowds of skeptics and critics, though he looked at the roads of ease and comfort when a cross beckoned, though he saw as has no other man the bottomless pit of seeming estrangement from the Father and cried, "My God, why?" yet the multitude could not sway him—the lesser life could not rule him—the cross could not frighten him. Because he overcame, "thanks be to God which giveth us the victory through our Lord Jesus Christ" (1 Cor. 15:57).

Thus, the second point has already been touched. He who *lives* the way, *points* the way for us. The way then becomes not so much a trail to be walked but a traveler who walks with us. This is the power of our gospel—not a path but a person, not a direction but a director, not a road but a Redeemer!

The story is told of a pilot who crash landed in the jungles of Burma. He was not seriously injured, and when a native came to aid him in traversing the jungle he was able to follow. But it was difficult trudging. The new friend had to hack and chop the denseness of the jungle growth with his knife so that they might walk. Not feeling altogether safe, the pilot asked, "Are you sure this is the way?" His rescuer replied: "There is no way. I am the way. Follow me!"

They are the words of another. "I am the way" (John 14:6). Behold, he goeth before you.

II

Christ goes before to strengthen us. The Christian way
is not an escape hatch that detours us from either responsibility or misfortune. Let us seek to develop these
two points, keeping the fact in mind that in both of
these particulars we have the promise of his nearness. "I
am with you alway" (Matt. 28:20).

Each of us is a God-called witness. It does not matter
where your particular field of service may be. You may
be God's voice at a medical center, department store,
service station, high school, living room. But wherever
there is a professing Christian, there should be one whose
life and voice testifies that Christ is near. Remember that
the youthful dynamic church of Acts was composed not
so much of professional preachers as loyal laymen. The
words "Christian" and "witness" are nearly synonymous.

When one surrenders his life to the Master and is
filled with the Christ-life then he in turn seeks to share
Christ's grace and glow with others. It is important to
note that you are not alone as you make your witness.
As in all of Christian experience, Christ goes before.

I recall once being the inspirational speaker for a lay
visitation program. The women's missionary group was
in charge of this witness group and I addressed their
gathered fellowship shortly before they embarked on
their afternoon of sharing the gospel. Among other things,
I encouraged them to pray. I told them Christ would use
them if they stayed constantly in his presence.

I shall never forget the comment of one rather timid

woman at the sharing hour that evening. "This is the first time I have ever done this sort of thing," she confessed. "Frankly, I was extremely apprehensive. Mr. Chappell urged us to pray and I must admit before I knocked at my first door, I prayed there would be no one at home." "Yet," she continued, after we had all had a laugh, "when our team was received into that home, I cannot explain it, but the atmosphere made it very plain that the Savior had entered before us." He always does. He always will.

If he goes before us in regard to our responsibilities, he goes before us when misfortunes come. Indeed Christ is always the first casualty when hearts are broken and lives are wrecked. The sensitive soul of the Master is ever grieved when any suffering child of his affection knows sorrow or loss.

That is why he wept over Jerusalem. He knew there was no continuing salvation for a city that refused his love. Ruin is always the end result of rejection. Disaster inevitably follows disobedience.

How it must have wounded his great heart when the wealthy man, whom we call the rich young ruler, declined to follow him. Our Lord knew that emptiness would be permanent when the youthful nobleman excluded his presence.

This is the real misfortune—not when some great tragedy strikes, but when we omit Christ from our lives so that we do not have his spirit within us when calamities do come.

I had an experience recently that brought rich treasure to my own spiritual coffer. A dear friend, one of the choice souls that I have known across a lifetime, had surgery for cancer. The night before the operation, this layman and I talked and prayed together. Upon leaving, I said, "Nick, I believe everything will be all right." His answer was immediate and unforgettable. "Wallace," he said humbly but confidently, "it will be all right if it is not all right." What can cancer do to a man in whose heart Christ has gone before?

III

Christ goes before to inspire us. Here we address ourselves to the basic relevance of the text.

"He goeth before you into Galilee," the angel said. It is a word of explanation concerning a living Lord, his constant availability and his unfailing power. This is why he inspires: He is living—he is present—he is adequate.

However, mark this fact. The disciples' first reaction to the news of Christ's resurrection was scarcely one of inspirational note. "With fear," says Matthew first (Matthew 28:8). "They were terrified and affrighted," echoes Luke (Luke 24:37). Do we understand what this means?

Whatever else may be its interpretation, it certainly indicates that the followers of Christ were hardly ready to set a world aright with courageous joy and inner peace. The Lord had told them he would go to a cross. This, then, was their future, too. How could they be happy in the clear consciousness that Calvary was an individual experience for each of them?

But he also told them he would return. And he had! If the grave could not hold him, it could not hold them. They remembered his words, "Because I live, you shall live also" (John 14:19).

And there had been another promise. "I will pray the Father, and he shall give you another Comforter, that he may abide with you for ever" (John 14:16).

Thus, even though suffering and persecution lay before them, they had a living Lord, an indwelling power, an eternal destiny. "He goeth before you." I submit, that is grounds for inspiration.

Bishop Paul Kern used to relate a very interesting experience. In the days of great football at Vanderbilt, there was a star tackle named Joe Prichard. At a YMCA conference Joe heard the appeal of Sherwood Eddie as the great Christian stressed the need for young Christian witnesses on college campuses. Joe volunteered as one of the workers. When the committee informed him that he was being sent to the University of Mississippi, Joe became frightened. "I was thinking that I would be sent to a small campus," he said. "I am afraid this is too large an assignment for me."

A member of the placement committee with unusual understanding felt he knew the answer to Joe's apprehension. "Joe," he asked, "would you be willing to go with Sherwood Eddie to the Ole Miss campus?" "Sir," he answered, "I would go anywhere with Sherwood Eddie."

Then that member of the committee said, "Joe, would you go with the one who has gone with Sherwood Eddie, even preceding him everywhere he has gone? That one is Jesus Christ!"

Young Prichard stood tall then in the realization that the Valiant Vanguard was his strength. Earnestly he answered, "Yes, I can go now!"

And in that faith, so can we!

9

The
Divine
Invasion

"They went out and preached everywhere, the Lord working with them and confirming the word by the miracles that endorsed it."

Mark 16:20, Moffatt

The minister and his Easter membership class were studying the Korean Creed together. We had arrived at what I consider to be the crowning summit of our faith: "We believe in the final triumph of righteousness, and in the life everlasting."

"Would someone like to state what this means to you?" I asked. A ten-year-old had her hand raised before I got the question out.

"Mr. Chappell," she said, "it means if you hold on to the hand of Jesus Christ, everything is going to come out right."

"They went out and preached everywhere, the Lord working with them and confirming the word by the miracles that endorsed it." It was as the disciples hooked their hearts to the risen Lord, life everlasting incarnate in Christ, that they made a wrong world right.

This, too, is our magnificent mission.

I

Note in the first place that the disciples went out proclaiming; that is *they tried*. Always the action ethic is part and parcel of our faith.

A preacher friend wrote a book some years ago entitled, *Love Is Something You Do*. He is right. Love, if it is genuine, must reach out with arms of compassion to bring the world to his cross and empty tomb.

They tried. They exerted an effort. They went about Jerusalem, then through Judea and Samaria and the Roman Empire. They had a love to give—a Christ to share—a world to win.

This effort of which we speak expresses itself in two ways: First, there is *a going out*. This is evident in our basic text. Observe also that they went out witnessing *everywhere*. Perhaps the hierarchy of the English Church felt that since John Wesley had been ordained at Oxford, he should preach at least within its borders. His answer was, "The world is my parish." This was the commitment of those who belonged to the fraternity of the Easter morning.

The church today must surrender to that same conviction. Whatever else the New Testament has to say about evangelism, it repeatedly points to such an aggressive and concerted offensive that nothing less than the whole world is included in its program.

If there is any doubt concerning this, look at the Scriptures:

"Jesus went about *all* the cities and villages . . . preaching the gospel of the kingdom" (Matt. 9:35).

"The Lord appointed seventy others and sent them . . . two by two, into *every* town and place," (Luke 10:1, RSV).

And the greatest words of all that addresses themselves to the divine invasion: "Go and make disciples of *all* nations" (Matt. 28:19, RSV).

The difference it would make today if our gathered fellowship appropriated this same life-giving dynamic of the amazing young church of Acts!!

A friend of our particular denomination was visiting recently in a large city in the northwest. He was eating breakfast in his hotel coffee shop when a layman of another denomination approached him and invited him to participate in worship services at the church he attended. Responding with appreciation, he inquired of his visitor if such procedures were not unusual. His inviter answered: "No, we are concerned with the spiritual welfare of the people coming into this city. This Sunday morning there are three hundred laymen walking the streets sharing Christ and encouraging people to attend church."

Trying. The action ethic of which we speak not only involves a going out but *a standing by.* There is the strategic witness we give right where are are. Jesus said, "You shall be my witnesses in Jerusalem and in all Judea and Samaria and to the end of the earth." But remember this: the disciples would have had little influence as they

shared the good news across the world if the people of
Jerusalem had not had faith in them at home.

I wonder that I have never heard a sermon preached
about Jesus in regard to this particular emphasis.

It has been suggested that Jesus was in his teens when
his father Joseph died. Let us imagine that his age was
eighteen. The Bible reminds us that our Lord had four
brothers. We do not know how many sisters he had—just
the plural is used. He might have had two or a half dozen.
As you will recall, it was the older brother who assumed
the leadership in the Jewish family when the father died.
So here was a young man caring for a large family.

We are told in the Scripture that Jesus began his
ministry when he was thirty and thirty-three when he
went to Calvary. If Jesus became the head of his home
at eighteen, this means that he spent four times as long
caring for his family as he did his Kingdom. What could
this mean but that in a very real sense the Master's home
was in fact his Kingdom?

I am thinking of a dear saint who could not go out.
She had to give her witness from her home. And since
she was a cripple, it was a sit-down witness. But what a
glory she shared. There is little telling how many phone
calls she made, how many devotional guides she sent, how
many buoyant notes she wrote. She was shut in by illness
but never shut out from goodness and every person who
came in contact with her touched her for their own heal-
ing.

II

The disciples not only tried, *they trusted*. This trust was born of two facts. First, they had confidence that Christ would *live in them*. Whatever else Pentecost means, the big truth is that the risen Lord was alive in the heart of every true follower.

Let me give this personal word. Recently while waiting for the car attendant to return my automobile at our parking lot, I was engaged in one of my more constant pasttimes. The day had brought many parish needs and pastoral burdens and I was quite fretful and worried. How could this situation be helped, I asked myself. Again, What might I do to remedy this problem? I wondered. To be perfectly honest, I was very close to becoming a bit of a wreck.

Suddenly the truth came with such a surprising joy that it fairly took my breath away. He had risen! The victory was mine! The Spirit reigned within! If Jesus had pushed the rock away from the tomb, he could push away the obstacles that blocked my spiritual vision—not only so, but he could use me to help him push away the difficulties through which some of his flock were passing. Or, if not dismiss these difficulties, give strength to those who faced them.

How often does our grace-conquering Master seek to make his living presence known to us! How many times does he strive to abide within us! I am so ashamed when

I think that most of my ministry has been spent in trying to work it out myself.

Not so the courageous young church of the Pentecost indwelling! Christ was no longer simply with them—he was in them. And these men of inner power knew that if their Lord had overcome death, there was no limit to his strength and no end to his love.

The second fact is that the disciples had confidence that Christ would *work through them*. Notice Mark's phrase, "the Lord working with them."

Again, I wish to testify to this fact. If I give a witness or preach a sermon or share a truth,—nothing. If the living Lord does it through me, watch out! Something is going to happen!

It happened to the Spirit-possessed of the New Testament fellowship. Sharing Christ with their realm, they revealed such love and joy—compassion and warmth—strength and peace—even their enemies had to admit they had turned the world upside down. (See Acts 17:6.)

It will happen today when and where his followers forget themselves into magnificent enterprises for the sake of the Kingdom.

I remember once, years ago, when my uncle, Clovis Chappell, and I were engaged in a series of services together. A lady approached him with glowing enthusiasm. "Oh, Dr. Chappell," she said, "you have been such a help to multitudes of people. There will be so many stars in your crown." He was kind in his response, but I will never forget his words to me. "It is a great thing," he said, "to know that we are witnesses of his gospel not to gain stars for our crowns but souls for his service."

This is not only possible, it becomes increasingly certain as we yield ourselves to be channels of the Christ way.

III

The disciples tried. The disciples trusted. Finally, in the fellowship of their risen Redeemer, *they triumphed.* We read that the Lord was "confirming the word by miracles."

Sometimes God works miracles through us that we never know about—we never see them. The witness is given. The seed is scattered. The gospel is shared. But the Holy Spirit moves upon the heart of the receiver and when the victory comes, we are not present to participate in its joy. Of course, we do not need to be. It is not necessary that an audience be available and certainly the sincere good news bringer does not want to applaud himself for bring the artery the Savior has used to bring a soul to himself.

"Dr. Livingstone led me to Christ," said Henry Stanley, "and he never knew he was doing it." And what matter if he didn't, so long as the glory was received and the mission accomplished.

Again, we read in Acts: "As a result of what the apostles were doing, the sick people were carried out in the streets and placed on beds and mats so that, when Peter walked by, at least his shadow might fall on some of them" (Acts 5:15, TEV).

Did the fishermen know what was happening? What does it matter so long as a shadow opens the door to the sunlight of another?

Other times, however, God allows us to see what he has done through us. He always knows when a blessing of this kind is needed.

Peter was the captain of the church militant. Andrew never had the name, the position, the adulation of his brother. Yet how quietly but thoroughly he must have rejoiced in the fact that "he first found his brother Simon and said to him, 'We have found the Messiah!'" (John 1:41, RSV).

During seminary days, I once preached for a friend of mine who was a minister in a city that was nationally infamous. A more prominent magazine referred to it as "the most wicked city in America."

There was an army base near by and several soldiers were in attendance at our services. I remember one evening a young corporal came to the church and when the invitation to accept Christ was given, he knelt at the altar and received the Savior.

More than ten years later, I received a letter from overseas. Part of it ran like this: "Shortly after turning my life over to Jesus Christ, I was released from the Army. I then finished college and went to seminary because God had called me to preach. I could not get my buddies in the Army out of my mind so I reenlisted—this time as a chaplain. I am now serving our Lord as chaplain in our most northern base in Thailand. This letter is to simply say that sometimes the seed sprouts."

"They went out and preached everywhere, the Lord working with them and confirming the word by the miracles that endorsed it."

The risen Christ will give the victory if we invade the world in the strength of His Spirit.

10

The
Dangerous
Delay

"After it was all over, Joseph (who came from Arimathaea
and was a disciple of Jesus, though secretly for fear of
the Jews), requested Pilate that he might take away
Jesus' body."

John 19:38, Phillips

Though this particular sermon does not deal specifically with our Lord's resurrection, we felt the need to share one message that we trust serves as a transition between darkness and dawn.

Look gain at the words: "After it was all over . . . Joseph . . . requested Pilate that he might take away Jesus' body."

"After"—that is a word that may carry in its usage the gloom of a shadow or the glory of the sun.

Look at it when it is glowing in the sunshine. *After* the sickness, he became well; *after* the sentence, he aided society; *after* the sorrow, he strengthened the disciples' faith as they faced difficult days. "Ye now therefore have sorrow," he said, "but I will see you again [after], and your heart shall rejoice." (John 16:22).

Now look at this word when it is mirrored in the shadows. *After* the redress, he betrayed God; *after* the remedy, he rejected righteousness; *after* the restoration,

117

he failed humanity.

And you will recall when our Lord talked to his followers about his death John said, "After this many of his disciples drew back and no longer went about with him" (John 6:66, RSV).

Even so, the truth of our text brings an overcast sky and a songless night. "After it was all over," . . . his aloneness, his denial, his betrayal, his suffering, his death . . . after, then Joseph came.

A minister told a pathetic incident that occurred in his community. There was a certain family which suffered, and unjustly so, because of the extreme miserliness of the head of the house. The man's wife, a devoted Christian, was not given money for new clothing, not even enough to purchase the fabric to make a new dress. She died even though quite young. The day after her funeral, the pastor went to see the farmer and found him beside her tomb. He was in the process of covering her grave with yards and yards of lace material. After!

There are three facts that I think should be brought to our attention as we anticipate the relevance of the text.

I

Sometimes meaningful experiences are thwarted or procrastinated and it is due to one of two factors. It is the fault of follower or leader.

If it is due to defective leadership, it may be because the one in authority is not clear in his presentation of intent. It was said of Lord Nelson that he always won his battles because he arrived at the scene of conflict early.

Listen to our Lord's clarion call as he initiated his kingdom: "The time is fulfilled and the kingdom of God is at hand." (Mark 1:15).

Rita Snowden has reminded us that the early preachers of America were called the "Now" men. Like their Lord, they were present inviters to the kingdom, believing in the words of Paul that "now is the accepted time."

But if we are not clear as to presentation—*when*, we also may not be clear as to intent—*what*. Now is the time to act but what specifically are we to do?

Again, Jesus was quite intelligible at this point. "Repent," he said, "and believe the gospel." So, too, the apostle from Tarsus did not lack lucidity at this point. "If thou shalt confess with thy mouth the Lord Jesus and shalt believe in thine heart that God hath raised him from the dead," he said, "thou shalt be saved." (Rom. 10:9).

The fact is that Jesus was all to clear in his language and actions. When he called the Pharisees "whitewashed tombs," they did not misunderstand his meaning. When he drove those who sold from the Temple, they knew exactly what he meant.

No! Great moments with Christ go unrealized because of failure to follow. The fault to be sure lay not with Christ but with Joseph.

Jesus told a story about a man who was going abroad and before leaving he summoned his servants and distributed his property to them. To one he gave five thou-

sand dollars. To another, two thousand dollars. The last
one received one thousand dollars. When the master
returned to settle the books, he called for his servants. The
one who had been given five thousand had increased it
to ten thousand. The one who had been trusted with
two thousand had raised it to four thousand. But the servant to whom one thousand had been given yielded no
accumulation whatsoever. Was this the fault of master
or servant? leader or follower? To ask this question, of
course, is to answer it.

II

Now how do we miss and why do we delay the supreme
experience of life: the encounter of the heart and Jesus
Christ? I think there are several reasons.

One reason must be because we do not recognize the
holy hour when it comes. You have to say one thing in
Peter's behalf before the coming of the Spirit. He knew
a great hour when it arrived. True, he often missed all
that these experiences with his Lord included and granted
that he did not always have the salt to back up his beliefs,
yet his soul knew that the mighty workings of God were
in operation.

"Master," he said during his Lord's transfiguration, "it
is good for us to be here." (Mark 9:5). And again, he declared, "Thou art the Christ, the Son of the living God."
(Matt. 16:16). It was his identification with the *moment*
and the *Master* that was gradually causing formation of
the *rock*.

The pathetic point of Henry James' very fine study *The Beast in the Jungle,* is that the great moment may go unidentified—unrealized. It is the story of a man who searches in vain for the love he feels that is waiting some-where and realizes too late that it was at his very door all the while, unheeded—unknown—unwanted.

"If thou knewest . . .," said Jesus to the woman at the well. But how often we do not!

Another reason that we miss or delay the paramount encounter is that there is no sign of joyful discovery in our faith. Do you recall our Lord's story of the sower? You will remember that the first seed that was sown was the only seed that did not sprout at all. It was scattered but it never grew.

Something like this happened when our Lord came to minister in his hometown. Listen to Matthew's touching commentary: "He did not many mighty works there be-cause of their unbelief." (Matt. 13:58). They had heard of his achievements but there was no eager anticipation, no radiant expectation at his arrival.

This is the cause of our missing the grandest in every area of existence. Some of us read the *Iliad* or the *Odyssey* and yawn. Keats met Homer and it changed his life.

Now we need to offer to the superior calls of the soul what one has referred to as "hospitality to the highest."

The last reason for missing or delaying has to be that we are fearful of acting. This, you know, is the reason John gives for Joseph's failure. Read again his rather pitiful word. "After this Joseph of Arimathaea, being a disciple of Jesus, but secretly, for fear of the Jews . . ."

If John was the author of the Fourth Gospel, as I believe he was, here is a man writing of fear who knows something about it. How cowardly had he and the others been during our Lord's arrest and trial.

Oh yes, the time was coming when they would stand, he and Simon, before the council with flags flying and grace glowing. Luke would tell us about it: "When they saw the boldness of Peter and John . . . they took knowledge of them that they had been with Jesus" (Acts 4:13). But this did not occur until their living Lord had transformed their timidity into trust and their fright into faith.

May God not allow us because of faintheartedness to miss the life that lifts and the stand that sways. I pray that I will not let cowardice keep me from being the deliverer of the only news that can redeem and remake this world.

My soul! Look at the avenues of approach where the gospel must be declared. Are all men really brothers? Dare one be ethical in his economics? Can community-life be Christian? Is the church a country club or a light-house? Can we not cry triumphantly at the scope of our witness as Martin Dibelius did of his in Germany, "We are living in the Acts of the Apostles, and oh, it is glorious!"

III

What is the result of acting "after"? What is the consequence of bringing flowers to the funeral instead of giving laurels to the living?

The first thing is that Joseph missed the joy he could have known in all-out commitment to Christ. There is a lot of difference, you know, between sharing a cause and requesting a body.

How many there are today that are missing the cheer of total allegiance because they have never stepped out of the shadows into the sunlight of his fullness.

I asked one recently who was searching for the way if she was willing to open the door and admit the seeking Savior. "With all my heart," was the reply. We never know this glorious gladness if our answer be less.

Then there was the omitted joy Joseph could have brought to others.

A man in Atlanta was soundly converted. After this experience, he began to make restitution in every way possible for all the wrong he had done. To the best of his ability he did this. But a bit later he stood by the grave of his son who had been killed in an accident while drunk and reflected upon the fact that it was under his tutelage he had started drinking. A friend nearby heard him utter this distressing word: "O God! I can't make this right."

They are all around us—these needy ones to whom the presence of Christ is unknown. Some are members of our family. Some are friends. Some are neighbors. Fulton Sheen says there are ten million men and women walking our American streets today groping after God. I believe this. Of course, there are millions who seem unconcerned, but others are earnestly striving to find meaning in life. Can they find it in the kind of witness you and I are giving them?

Finally, there was the neglected joy Joseph could have brought to his Lord. We need Christ's companionship. But make no mistake about it, the Master needs our companionship.

"Couldest not thou watch one hour," he asked his disciples while he was enduring the agony of Gethsemane alone (Mark 14:37).

What encouragement it would have been to Jesus if Joseph had come from his place of hiding. What courageous cheer it would have given Christ for this secret disciple to have taken his stand.

I can picture in my imagination the man from Arimathaea coming forward at the Master's trial. Christ is without a friend. A weak man is his judge. Corrupt men are his accusers. The howling mobs are his critics. All are against him. Suddenly when the sentence is passed and they are preparing to lead him on the death march to Golgotha, one comes and pushes a soldier aside and grips the arm of Christ. The crowd becomes suddenly hushed. They recognize this man at once. He is no Simon of Cyrene—a stranger in their midst. He is one of their own—a member of the Sanhedrin, wealthy and respected. He is speaking now. His voice is clear. His words are sure. "If you take my Lord, take me! I am one of his."

But instead, Joseph came after. Yet, remember that though he was tardy, though he was late, though it was *after*, he came. Have you? Will you?

Author's Personal Word

On the eve of the publication of this manuscript, my uncle, Dr. Clovis Chappell, made his victorious transition from earth to heaven.

For twenty-four years we had the most amazing relationship I have ever known. We preached together—traveled together—prayed together—lived together.

I cannot put into words how I miss him. But even the emptiness is triumphant because of his life and witness and legacy.

We often discussed this particular manuscript, "When Jesus Rose." We shared the Scriptures and ideas on numerous occasions.

"Buddy," he said to me one day, "in my opinion this is the best thing you have ever done." I am not relating this to brag on the book, I think I know my own limitations better than anyone. But the resurrection was something he believed in—perhaps more than any gospel certainty. I must confess my confidence in this fact too.

Because of his assurance and influence and love, though I must assume responsibility for the shortcomings, this is really his book.